Girls

J.J. Smiley

Published by J.J. Smiley, 2022.

While every precaution has been taken in the preparation of this book, the publisher assumes no responsibility for errors or omissions, or for damages resulting from the use of the information contained herein.

GIRLS

First edition. November 18, 2022.

Copyright © 2022 J.J. Smiley.

ISBN: 979-8215563489

Written by J.J. Smiley.

Table of Contents

A Knack for Trouble Chapter 1

Christine had a knack. Unfortunately, it was a knack for drawing unwanted attention anywhere she went. Her girlfriend, Jennifer, told her it was the way she dressed, clothes too tight in all those places that people take notice. Another girlfriend, Jackie, said it was her smile, she smiled at everyone she met, and it sparkled. But, on the other hand, she sarcastically thought it might be her engaging conversation.

Christine Baker, at 26, was slender and adequately blessed with a fulfilling 'D' cup. The natural blond hair was also a compliment. At five foot four and 120 pounds, she was more than attractive, and she was easily the victim of ogling stares by both men and women. After a few adult years with this type of body, it was no surprise that self-defense classes took place three times a week at a karate dojo. After a year, she was at the head of her class and often took over for the instructor, Steward, who was himself, a handsome, athletic figure. She thought, at times, Stew would be an admirable choice as a boyfriend, but as time went by in class, it became evident that he had his agenda, and it didn't include women, but he was the best Sensei in the business.

It had been a grueling sweat filled two hours, and the class was finally over for Monday.

"Bye, Stew, see you on Wednesday," she said at the door while leaving.

"Sure thing! See you then," Stew replied.

She shut the front door of Steward Nakamoto's dojo and proceeded to the parking lot alongside the cinder block building. She had been the last to leave but was confident her skill would keep her safe. How insightful can one get? Pulling the keys out of her purse, she unlocked the car door. Someone grabbed her arm and spun her around.

"Well, pretty lady, where do you think you're going?"

"Home," she said as she delivered a swift knee to the stranger's groin.

Not wanting him to recover too quickly, she finished off with a spinning kick that turned him to the left and slammed him in the head with her purse, turning him to the right. One last kick to the side and the stranger fell unconscious. Looking around, she saw no one coming to her aid nor anyone who could be a witness. However, rather than leave the scene, she felt she should at least get this jerk some medical attention. After all, she did provide the injuries.

She pulled out her phone, which had survived inside the purse, and dialed 911. While she waited, she decided to check out this guy's identification. She pulled out his wallet and found his driver's license. Jason Krepki was the name she found; 25 years old, lives at 21314 Oak Drive, five foot eleven inches, eyes and hair brown, and 185 pounds. She put the license back in the wallet and found some money. With only the slightest hesitation, she pulled out a couple of twenties to cover the time it was going to take her to press charges against this guy.

The police arrived; two cops, one older and one younger, both clean, crisp, and good-looking gentlemen. They took her statement. Likewise, the ambulance showed up. EMTs put Jason on a gurney. The cops handcuffed one of his wrists to the sidebar and helped shove him into the truck.

"Are you hurt in any way, young lady?" the younger cop said.

Before she could answer, the older cop said, "For now, we're assuming you are the victim and not the assailant, but judging from the condition of the other guy, I'm not entirely sure."

"Well, this is my car, and you can talk to the building owner, and you'll find out I just left my class. So, where's this guy's car, and from where did he come? And remember, I'm the one that called 911!"

"Well, ma'am, we would have asked him, except he was unconscious."

With this, she felt a pang of guilt, but only for a second.

"Please stay in town; we'll need you at the station later," said the older cop.

"Sure, I'll be here. Just call me when you need me."

With this episode over, at least for now, Christine headed for home. Driving through traffic to her downtown loft, she thought about the day. It was ho-hum at work, and the martial arts class afterward was challenging but average at best. However, the parking lot affair was pretty commendable, although, thinking back, the guy didn't put up much of a fight. "Holy crap," she thought, "did I react too fast?" But, on the other hand, maybe the guy wasn't a mugger. "Well, if he wasn't, he needed a lesson in manners, and I gave him a lesson he won't soon forget," she mumbled.

She arrived at her apartment and was opening the door when Jennifer, her girlfriend, whom she worked with and who lived down the hall, was coming home.

"Oh, hi Chris, I was going to call you. A guy stopped by the office; I think his name was Jason, and he said he was a relative of your stepmom. He seemed really nice and wanted to talk to you.

He said his mom, your aunt, was really sick and wanted you to stop by and see her."

Christine's heart sank.

"Thanks, Jenn. I didn't see him. Maybe he'll catch up to me later. I'll call my mother and find out what's what. Talk to you later."

Chris got inside and closed the door and locked it. She fell back against the door, looked up, and said, "Oh my God!" She dug out her phone and dropped half the stuff in her purse on the floor while doing so.

"Hi, mom; how are things?" She stammered while trying to remain calm.

Judy, her mother, had been close friends. So, it was no surprise for Christine to call just to shoot the breeze. But, as far as her mother was concerned, this was just a casual call.

"Hi darling, I was waiting till I was sure you were home to call you. My sister Elaine has been extremely sick, and I'm going to visit her in Chicago. So, I was wondering if you could stop by and look in on your dad from time to time?"

"Well, sure, Mom! Say, did I ever visit Aunt Elaine when I was younger? I don't remember much about her."

"I only took you to visit her once. Her husband had died some months before, and her only son, Jason, was away at military school."

"Oh yeah, I never met her son, did I?"

"No, but he was about a year younger than you are, anyway."

They continued to chit-chat for another twenty minutes. Chris did not want to rush her mom but knew she needed to get to the hospital ASAP. Chris finally hung up and went straight to the shower. Between two hours of training and the parking lot adventure, she had a lot of cleaning up to do. She got dressed and put on her makeup. She wanted to look as good as possible; maybe the apologizing would come easier.

Chapter 2

Christine arrived at the hospital. She entered the lobby and asked for Jason Krepki's room.

"I'm sorry, but he is in isolation and can't receive visitors," said the information clerk in a matter-of-fact response.

"But I'm family."

Sorry, he can't have visitors right now. Maybe later." The clerk stated emphatically and without the least amount of compassion. The nurse used HIPPA regulations as a way to curtail any further conversation.

"Well, thanks anyway."

The nurse merely shrugged. Undaunted, Chris left the lobby and headed around back to the emergency area. The room was crowded and chaotic, which was her hope. She slipped in and wandered around until she found a door marked 'storage.' She slipped inside and grabbed a white lab coat. She stepped out of the room and saw a stethoscope and a badge with a neck strap hanging conveniently on a hook. She put both around her neck. She looked as much the part as anyone on the floor.

Chris went down a few halls until she found the sign that said, 'police lockup, authorized personnel only,' she went in. Wearing the frock, she blended in easily. She grabbed a clipboard and looked in the rooms. There was only one police officer standing in the hall. Chris finally saw Jason through a room window. He was being interrogated by two men who were apparently detectives. She couldn't hear what they were saying, but they were leaving. She turned into an alcove in the hallway and stared down at her clipboard. The detectives passed behind her, none the wiser. They left the lockup area, and she nonchalantly walked into Jason's room.

Jason looked up and saw the fake doctor. He knew exactly who she was and tried desperately to jump out of bed. His sheets and ice pack went flying. The handcuffs, still attached, kept him in the bed.

"Jason, please try to calm down, I now know who you are, and I'm terribly sorry. Please forgive me. I know now I overreacted. Jason seemed to relax just a little. He held on to his genitals as he moaned and settled himself into the bed. Chris picked the ice pack off the floor and handed it to Jason. He placed it on his groin and moaned again.

"Maybe I was too forward when I met you, but I thought you might have remembered me from a photo or something. It was more my fault than yours," he said in a weak voice.

Sitting in the bed, Jason looked terrible. His right eye was pretty much swollen shut, the left side of his head had three stitches, and his chest was taped to keep the broken rib in place. He might as well have been hit by a car.

Chris had tears in her eyes. "I'm so sorry," she repeated.

"Jason, didn't you explain this to the police."

"Chris, I have a tainted past. I was so bad my mother sent me away to a military academy. To make a long story short, the cops didn't believe me."

Chris pulled her cell phone out and stepped into the hallway. She called the number the cop had given her. She tried to explain what had happened, and it quickly became a too unrealistic a story. So, without any further explanation, she merely said she was dropping any charges, and that was that.

She went back into the room. She looked at Jason and realized that he was not a bad-looking guy without the bruising and bandages. A few minutes later, an officer came in, took off the handcuffs, and left without saying anything.

"I guess you're a free man. I hope you can see your way to forgive me," Chris said.

"Yeah, sure, I was on vacation when I came down here, and the ribs won't cause me much pain. I'm a stockbroker in Chicago, so I can survive just sitting for a while."

"If you give me your keys, I'll arrange to bring your car to my place until you're up and around. Here are my phone number and address."

"Great, and thanks," he described the car and where it was parked and tossed her the keys. She laid her address on the bedtable.

"You got your phone, right? I'm sure you need to call your wife and tell her what an idiot you have for a cousin."

"No wife to call. Maybe I'll call my mother later tonight. She's been very sick, and I need to check on her."

Chris looked at him again. "Trim, sweet face, stockbroker, no wife; I hope he feels better soon," she thought.

"Ok, call me tomorrow, let me know how you're feeling. Good night," Chris said while leaving.

"Goodnight," he called out as she left the room.

Chapter 3

The following day Chris was up early to do a few chores before work. It was Tuesday, and the weekend seemed too far away, and she was looking forward to the action the weekend would bring. She had her first coffee and was ready to head out. She saw the red Audi A5 parked in the apartment parking lot next to hers. She had called her girlfriend Jackie last night and, after picking her up, had Jackie drive Jason's car to her apartment. It was a nice-looking car; Jackie said it drove like a dream.

Before work, Christine headed to the store and was shopping for some wine for the evening when she ran into Jennifer.

"Morning, Chris,"

"Oh, hi, Jenn," Chris replied

"Chris, did you meet up with your cousin yet?"

"Well, yeah, but you won't believe what happened."

Chris divulged an overview of the events from the evening before. Jenn was stunned but immediately probed for more detail. Jenn had already met Jason and assessed him as good-looking and worthy of a roll in the hay.

"No time right now, Jenn. Call Jackie and see if she's free on Friday night, and you and she come over for some wine, and I'll fill in the details."

"You bet I'll be over with or without Jackie. But I really want to hear more of this story."

"Ok, later," Chris said and headed for the checkout. She put her few items on the counter for the clerk. The clerk smiled at her and then looked behind her and said, "Morning, Ted."

"Morning, Susan," Ted replied.

Chris immediately recognized the voice and turned to verify what she was thinking. The young cop she had met yesterday was there, but this time dressed in a t-shirt and shorts with a blue hoodie. She thought he was handsome yesterday in his uniform but was surprised at how good-looking he was in casual dress as well. He still stood out as trim figured with well-cut muscles, not too bulky.

"Fancy meeting you here, officer," Chris said.

"Morning, how are you today? I know we've only met in an official capacity. So, hi, I'm Ted Shontz; just call me Ted but please, not 'Teddy,' and you are?"

"Right! Right!" Chris said, still a little flustered. "I'm Christine Baker; just call me Chris."

"Well, nice to meet you, Chris."

"Likewise,"

"Ted, do you come here often?"

"No, I just transferred to this precinct a few weeks ago, so I'm new to the area."

Thinking quickly, Ted had mentioned that 'he' moved and not 'I moved my family' Chris casually said, "I'm having a little get-together on Friday night; are you free?"

"Sure! What time?"

"How about eight-ish?"

She knew he would have her address from the police report but jotted it down and handed it to him anyway. "Great! See you then,"

"Right," he said with a smile.

Chris almost tingled on her way to the car. At work, Chris sat at her desk. She had clients to call and orders to place, but her mind was on other things, two handsome guys on the same day, and it was hard to focus. It would be a long day, and so would Wednesday, Thursday, and Friday. Much to Jennifer's consternation, Christine kept mum about the Jason story. At the end of the workday, Chris gathered her things and told her co-workers to have a good weekend. She decided to skip Karate class and headed home to clean the house for the upcoming get-together. Eight-ish could not come soon enough.

Chapter 4

Jenn arrived first, and Jackie a few minutes later. Chris gave up some of the parking lot event details and then added the store encounter with Ted. The doorbell rang, and they all stared at each other and smiled.

"Hi Ted, come in."

"Hi, Chris," Ted said while handing her a bottle of wine.

"How nice, thanks," Chris said. "These are my friends Jenn and Jackie."

Ted smiled and shook hands with each girl.

"Have a seat, and I'll pour some wine."

Ted sat at the end of the couch, and Jackie, the more forward of the three, plopped down close to him. She inhaled his cologne and mentally approved, slightly musky but subtle and indeed arousing. Jenn seated herself on the opposing sofa and, not to be outdone by Jackie, crossed her legs and allowed her skirt to ride up higher on her thigh than would seem modest. Chris remained standing and sipped her wine, thinking, "look at those two hussies. I hope they don't embarrass themselves."

The conversation was light, and Jenn and Jackie both talked about their recent lives and how they had met Chris. Ted also explained his passion for law enforcement and how he had moved here to get more experience. He told them how, when he was a child, his parents had been murdered during a robbery attempt while they were shopping in a jewelry store. He was now dedicated to catching bad guys. After hearing this heart-wrenching story, all three girls collectively gave a quiet sigh.

"Well, just keep in mind that we're the good guys, and I'm more than willing to prove it," Jackie said provocatively while licking the edge of her wine glass.

Chris could see that Jackie was making Ted a little nervous with her tone of the conversation and invited her to help bring the hors-d'oeuvres from the kitchen. Jenn quickly took her place on the couch, closer than Jackie had been; she also liked the smell of his cologne. However, she was less provocative than Jackie in her conversation. Jenn told of her education in college as a design major and how disappointed she was not to be able to land a decent job in this arena.

Chris returned from the kitchen with Jackie, each carrying a platter of finger foods. Christine was noticeably upset with Jenn's position on the couch. Jenn noticed Chris's frown and moved a few inches away from Ted. They all ate as they continued to grill Ted on his childhood life. Ted related his life growing up with his aunt and uncle as an orphan in Ohio. The evening was kept light, and Chris manipulated the topics and seat positions to keep Ted comfortable. Everyone had been up early, and this was the end of another workday.

After midnight, Jenn was yawning, and Jackie was exasperated that she could not get closer to Ted on the couch. Jenn said she needed to call it a night and prodded Jackie to agree. Finally, they both left, and Ted felt it was time for him to get home. Chris was not surprised that this straight-up, handsome cop would be anything less than a gentleman.

"It was great for you to invite me over. Maybe I could take you out to dinner tomorrow if you're not too busy."

"That would be great, Ted. What time?"

"Is seven too early?"

"Perfect"

"Ok, I'll pick you up at seven then,"

Chris closed the door and got her glass. She sipped the last of her wine while thinking about what she would wear. "That nice black outfit keeps me supported and is easy to get in and out of when needed," she thought out loud.

The wine let her sleep well, and her dreams were erotic, to say the least. Jason was on one side, and Ted was on the other. They were both enjoying her riches, and she was enjoying theirs. It was one of those dreams that you just don't want to leave, but something forces you back to reality, and you're not happy with whatever or whoever brought you back.

"Damn alarm clock!" she shouted and threw it across the room; she tried desperately to crawl back into her dream. The clock was still ringing, and she had to crawl across the bedroom to shut it off. Sitting on the floor by where the clock had landed, she decided she might as well get dressed.

She was just going into Stew's Dojo studio when she saw Jason pull up in his Audi. He parked and came in.

"Jason! How are you feeling? How did you get the car?" She looked him over and saw that his swollen eye was now open, but his face was still bruised.

"Much better, thanks. I had an Uber drop me off, and I had a spare key. I went to your apartment for the other, and obviously, you weren't home. So, I thought I'd try here."

"Well, ok, the other key is still at home. Can you come over in a while? I'm almost done here."

"Sure, sure! How about two hours from now?"

"Perfect!"

Jason turned and walked away. "Cute butt," she thought as she finished her workout, and headed home. Two hours later, Jason knocked on her apartment door.

Chapter 5

"Hi Jason, come in. How's Aunt Elaine?"

"Not well, I'm afraid. I have some business to finish up, and then I need to head back to Chicago soon."

"Well, at least let me make you a snack before you head back."

"Thanks; I could use a bite to eat."

"What would you like to drink?"

"Whatever you're having."

"How about some chilled Riesling? It goes well with the turkey sandwiches I'm making."

"Sounds great."

Chris poured the wine and returned to the counter to slice the turkey breast she had bought yesterday. While her head was turned, Jason picked up his glass and added the Ketamine to her drink. She finished making the sandwiches and brought them to the table.

"Here's to you," Jason said, lifting his glass in the air and then taking a sizeable gulp.

"Same to you," Chris did the same and took a goodly sized drink.

"Wow, that tasted horrible. Did your wine taste ok?" she said, feeling a little dizzy. She took another swallow, and Jason smiled at her as she stumbled to the couch, holding her head.

"I don't know what to think, and I really can't think, Jason. I'm sorry, I need to lie down."

"Sure, let me help you."

Chris was unconscious now, and Jason carried her into the bedroom.

"I was just going to kill you, but after that beating you gave me, I think I will have a little fun first."

Jason undressed Chris slowly for his own perverted satisfaction. He pulled her pants off, then her blouse. She could only moan with little strength to fend off his hands. He took her panties off and looked at the soft blond hair of her mound. He fondled it but only for a moment. Next, he unclasped her bra and pulled it off slowly as the two perky breasts spilled out. He pinched each nipple, and she simultaneously moaned with delight and loathing rejection. He saw the lubricant on the dresser and flipped her over in the bed. He applied the lube to her lower area and to his still bruised and flaccid shaft. He was having difficulty getting hard and, in frustration, spanked her cheeks several times with his open hand, hoping to stimulate himself into an erection. Chris was now moaning and crying. Still unable to achieve an erection, Jason decided to lubricate his hand. "This will be my revenge for the ass beating you gave me; after that, you're just going to die. With you gone, my mother's estate will go to me, not some idiot bitch."

The doorbell rang.

Jason stopped, perplexed at what to do next. The bell rang again.

"Chris, I know you're in there; I saw you come in; I need your help. Get off the toilet. I'll wait." Jenn rang the doorbell again.

Wiping the lubricant from his hands, Jason answered the door, not opening it completely. "Hi, Jenn. Chris wasn't feeling good, so she laid down for a while."

"Oh yeah, you're the cousin, Jason; God, I'm sorry I was so loud. Chris is the only one that's handy at fixing things around here. My oven won't light, and I'm trying to bake a cake."

"Maybe I can help."

"Could you? That would be great!"

Jason unlocked the door mechanism and closed it behind him, following Jenn down the hall. They went into Jenn's apartment; she showed Jason what the problem was and turned away to move the cake pan aside. With her back turned, he put her in a chokehold with his right arm and pulled it tighter with his left hand. She was struggling, and he gave her a hard twist. There was a cracking noise, and her arms drooped to her side; Jason held his hold for a few more seconds, then let go. Jenn, with her neck broken, fell to the floor, dead.

Jason wiped down everything he had touched and backed away through the door, closing it gently. He walked calmly back to Chris's apartment and saw the open door. Now fear and panic ran through him. He went inside and found the apartment empty. He went back into the hall and checked around all the corners; the hall was empty. He ran back to the elevator near Jenn's door. He hadn't heard the elevator while in Jenn's room and realized there must be a stairway. Jason ran to the other end of the hall, pulled the stairway door open, and entered the stairwell.

He could hear a commotion from below and went down the stairs cautiously. Two stories down, he saw Chris wrapped in a bed sheet, lying on the floor, being attended to by two guys in coveralls.

"Chris, what happened? Are you alright?" Jason feigned concern, thinking he could talk his way out of the situation.

Chris looked up in horror and screamed, "That's him!" as loud as she could.

The two maintenance men looked up at Jason, and each pulled a good-sized wrench from the pouches hanging from their belts.

Jason, in a panic, rushed the men. The first one sidestepped Jason and plowed into the second. The first one swung his wrench at Jason but, being off balance, missed. Jason pinned the second man to the wall and knew the other guy would try to get at him. He pulled the man off the wall, turned him to use as a shield, and then pushed the man toward the other attacker. Both the maintenance men were recovering their stance, and Jason decided to get out while he could. He ran out the stairwell door.

Chapter 6

Chris was weeping convulsively on the floor, trying to pull the bed sheet tighter around her. One of the maintenance men returned through the stairwell door after chasing Jason.

"He got away, sorry." The other man, who had been trying unsuccessfully to calm Chris down, said,

"We got a good look at him, don't worry. I'll call 911, and the cops will get this guy.

"Oh, God! Please, I think he's done something to Jenn," Chris cried.

"I know her, I'll go check her apartment, and you call 911," he said to his partner.

Returning after a few minutes with a horribly stricken look on his face, he looked at Jenn and just shook his head.

"The police will be here in a few minutes," the man said.

"I'll wait in the lobby till the cops get here," said the other.

The police arrived a few minutes later. Ironically one of the officers was the same older man that was at the parking lot incident. Chris sat on the couch, still wrapped in the bed sheet. The other police officer was downstairs taking statements from the maintenance men. Another set of officers were in Jenn's room with the coroner.

Chris tearfully related how she thought she must have been drugged. "I was in a stupor, and then I thought I heard Jenn at the door, then he left, and I tried to get up and fell a few times. I pulled the sheet around me and went to get help. I decided not to go towards the elevator and started down the stairs; at the bottom, the maintenance men found me." She couldn't go further.

The officer told her to rest briefly and stepped out into the hall. His regular partner, Ted, said to him that he and this girl were having a date tonight. So, he phoned Ted and asked him to come by and help settle this girl's nerves.

A little while later, detectives showed up, and Chris had to go over the story again. She was a little more composed and had dressed in slacks and a blouse. Telling the story, she remembered Jason saying something about her aunt's estate and how Jason had been cut out of the will and everything was being left to her.

"Well, that covers motive, and I'm afraid your friend just happened in at the wrong time," the detective said.

"But why did he have to kill her?"

"She would have been a witness, and he was coming back to finish you off when he was done with her."

"God! Jenn saved my life."

"Her involvement gave you enough time to recover and get out; you're a pretty lucky young lady."

"What happens now?"

"Well, we'll start the manhunt for Jason, but I'm afraid he may still see you as a roadblock to his mother's money; we'll need to assign..." Just then, Ted showed up. "Assign someone to..." he tried to finish again.

"It's ok, Teds here," Chris embraced him, and Ted felt just a little awkward but returned the hug warmly. "I won't mind the stakeout duty if it's alright with you."

"I suppose not. I'll call the captain and explain the circumstances."

With that settled, Chris sat with Ted and retold the whole story again. Ted explained that he would not leave her side until Jason was caught. As reassuring as it was, she started to cry, thinking about her friend Jenn.

"Try to relax a little," Ted said gently. "Just lay here on the couch, and

I'll make some dinner if you don't mind me poking around your kitchen."

"Sure, go ahead, I'm exhausted, but I think I can rest as long as you're here."

'

She laid down on the couch. Barely a minute went by before she was asleep. Ted set about quietly working the kitchen. He found a box of spaghetti and started the water boiling. Next, he saw the Ragu and a few spices to go with it. He got the lettuce cleaned and chopped and found the cherry tomatoes, dressing, and croutons. Ted set the table, rinsed the spaghetti, and heated the sauce. He got everything into bowls and washed the pots and pans.

Chris had only slept a little more than an hour, but it was a good deep, undisturbed sleep. The only thing that woke her was the aroma of the sauce Ted was heating. He saw her on the sofa as she stretched while awakening. Her arms stretched out, and she pulled her blouse tightly to her chest, her nipples erect as the fabric pulled across them. She caught Ted blushing, and he turned away. "Dinner and modesty, is this guy not the greatest?" she thought.

"I didn't wake you, did I? You were really sleeping soundly."

"No, you're fine, but I'm starving, and everything smells great; let's eat."

Chris had a delightful selection of wine, and Ted pulled out a nice Chianti and poured two glasses before sitting down across from her.

"You're the best, Ted! I'm happy you're here, more than you can imagine."

"I'm only sorry about the circumstances. I'll be honest, and after our date, I was hoping you would have invited me up for a nightcap."

"Believe me, provided you didn't slurp your food; I had every intention of inviting you up." Ted flushed again, his cheeks lighting up like a traffic signal.

They finished dinner with small talk, each giving up little pieces of their background and childhood. Ted told Chris to lay back down and relax while he did the dishes. Chris leaned back and watched this guy wash, rinse, dry, and put away the silverware and every dish and glass.

"Ted, do you do laundry?" Chris asked, smiling.

"Yes, but no windows," Ted replied, laughing.

They spent the evening watching TV and chatting about their future. They both had an overwhelming sensual desire but were hesitant to share openly, especially under the circumstances, and neither wanted to appear too forward. The TV watching was running late, and Ted suggested they call it a night. He would sleep on the couch and her in her room. She fell asleep slowly, wishing he would come into her room. She fell lazily to sleep with this thought in her head.

In the dark, Chris could feel Ted's soft boyish fingers slowly massaging her vagina. She pulled his face to hers and felt his tongue go deep into her mouth; she happily returned the favor. He pulled his face away, cupped her breast, and lifted it to his mouth; his sucking was soft and gentle, bringing her higher and higher to fulfillment. Chris spread her legs and beckoned him in; he pushed deep into her wetness on top of her. He pulled her over and put her on top, and her own weight caused his manhood to push deeper inside. Ted held her breasts and, with his thumb and forefinger, rolled the tips of her nipples and then pinched hard. She winced and woke up. Looking around in the dark and feeling around, in the bed, beside her, she found nothing. No one was in the room except her.

Chapter 7

Chris got up the next morning and quietly went to the kitchen to make coffee. On the way, by the couch, she looked down at Ted, who seemed too big to be sleeping on it. Ted started to turn over, and she stopped in mid-stride, trying not to wake him. The covers took another turn, and a beautiful bum became uncovered; she shivered with delight over this voyeur spectacle.

She tiptoed the rest of the way to the kitchen and started the coffee. She sat at the table in her robe, watching Ted and mulling all the things he had done for her, certainly more than you'd ever get on a first date.

The coffee finished with a noisy whoosh as the last of the water steamed through. Between the aroma of the coffee and the steamboat symphony, he was awake. He didn't notice her at the table, and when he stood up, he made a full stretch with arms up toward the ceiling and legs apart. All the covers fell off. He looked around and saw Chris.

"Damn," he said as he grabbed a sheet to cover himself. "Sorry for the language, Chris; you took me by surprise."

"I think that's a delightful way to say good morning," Chris chuckled.

Ted didn't have a robe, so he wrapped the sheet around himself, grabbed his clothes, and headed for the bathroom. Chris made some eggs and bacon and was ready to serve breakfast by the time he finished. He could only shower. He hadn't brought any toiletries. Opening the bathroom door, the smell from the kitchen made his stomach growl. She had breakfast on the table and was pouring coffee when he arrived. They ate together again, chatting and defining what they would do during the day. Chris's robe was loosely tied. It parted a few times during breakfast. Just enough to be tantalizing but not lude. She knew it was happening but wanted Ted to get the drift. She was not a nun, and it's ok to make a pass.

"You know, Chris. I've been thinking. Maybe it would be better if we stayed at my place till they find Jason. He knows where you live, so let's not tempt fate."

"Sure, no problem, Ted. I'll grab a few things, and we can go whenever you want."

"I was told Jenn's funeral is on Tuesday, so bring some clothes for that," Ted reminded her.

At this thought, Chris hesitated. Then, filled with guilt, tears began pouring out. She leaned against the wall, and Ted came over and put his arms around her.

"None of this is your fault, Chris. Remember, you're not the bad guy here."

The first thing on the agenda was a trip to his house. He lived in a three-story apartment building much like Chris's but with two bedrooms. He unlocked the door and beckoned her in, and she turned in a circle inspecting the large living room. "Strictly masculine, completely male," she thought to herself. The living room walls were decorated with sports team logos, all leather sofas, chairs, and the biggest TV screen she had ever seen. In the corner were an elliptical machine and a weight bench with several sized barbells on a holding rack. The bedrooms were ample, and a moderately sized bathroom was set between them. One of the bedrooms held a king mattress. "That's an awful big bed for a single guy," Chris said.

"Long story short, you know how furniture salesman can talk you into upgrading?"

"Yeah, been there, done that,"

"This is your room. It's a double bed, is that ok?"

"Look at me, this will be just fine!"

Chris unpacked her clothes. When she finished, she met him in the kitchen. Ted was going through the cupboards and frig.

"I don't think I have enough food for guests. Do you mind if we go shopping before we do anything else?"

"Well, let's do it quick. I try not to shop on an empty stomach, and right now, I'm starving."

They left and went to the apartment parking lot. Jason spotted a dark Audi, which was unfamiliar. Chris got in the car, and Ted closed the door behind her while saying he had to check the trunk. He rifled a few things around while calling in his suspicions to a detective. He didn't want to spook Chris.

The trip to the market was short, and Ted kept his eye out for anyone that might be tailing them. His phone rang. The detective on the other end told him that the car in the apartment lot was not the suspect's car.

"Thanks," Chris overheard the detective.

"What's that all about?"

"I saw a car in my lot that matched Jason's. I phoned it in while I was in the trunk. I didn't want you to be worried."

"Do you really think he would come after me? After all, you guys have all the information on him. How could he even move without you seeing him?"

"There's an All-Points Bulletin out on him, but this isn't a cop show. People can get away with a lot, there are tens of thousands of cars moving around, and other parts of your job have to be focused on as well. Besides Jason's psychotic, he's wanted for murder already and doesn't even realize that his inheritance is already jeopardized."

"So, I'm still in jeopardy."

"I'm afraid so! That's why I'm assigned to your case."

Chris wondered if that was the only reason Ted was so nice to her. But, now that she thought about it, was she just another job assignment? She was silent the rest of the way to the store.

Chapter 8

They pulled up in the store parking lot. It was still early in the day, and the lot had only twenty or thirty cars. They got a spot not far from the door. After shopping for a half hour, they returned to the car. Ted was pushing the cart, and Chris was next to Ted when the black sedan came rushing up behind them. Ted was still on alert and heard the car first. He grabbed Chris and pulled her back roughly, causing her to fall to the pavement. The vehicle hit the shopping cart and sent it flying in the air. Still accelerating, the car sped out of the lot. Chris looked up from the pavement to see Ted standing with his service revolver pointed at the speeding vehicle. He was now pulling his phone out to call in.

"Why didn't you shoot?" Chris asked.

"Look across the street, where the exit is; people are waiting for the bus. A miss or a ricochet would have sent a bullet in their direction. I keep telling you; this is not TV or a movie. There's no glamour, and it's not action-packed. But it is dangerous, and Jason needs to be off the street."

"Yeah, you're right, Ted; let's go!"

"We'll wait till the squad car gets here, then recover what we can from the cart. After that, I want the squad to follow us home and add extra surveillance at the apartment."

Back at his apartment, Ted watched as the police car was slowly passing by; it would do this every fifteen to thirty minutes for the next 24 hours. He told Chris what was going on, and she looked very relieved.

"Ted, I've got a funeral on Tuesday, and I can't afford to be off work. What am I going to do?"

"You can't let this change you. You'll go on as usual. I'll be with you the whole time, and I promise not to be obtrusive while you're at work."

They ate a light Sunday evening dinner. Chris watched TV while Ted exercised on the ecliptic. Chris had calmed down considerably and was aware of Ted working up a light sweat on the machine. He wasn't paying attention to her, but she studied him intently, watching his muscles flex as he pumped away.

Ted finished and was wiping his face with a cloth when he brought the towel down from his face. Chris was standing in front of him, close. She took the towel from him and wiped his neck and arms; she didn't say a word, just smiled. She grabbed his t-shirt at the sides and pulled it up over his head. Ted did not resist. She rubbed her hands over his chest, then up to his neck. He still did not resist. Finally, she put her hands behind his neck and pulled him into her face. She kissed him long and hard; her tongue explored his mouth, and he hers. Ted not only did not resist but succumbed to her charms and his own reserved feelings about her.

"I've been waiting for you, in my mind, in my soul; this is much more than payback for all you've done for me." She said softly.

"I feel the same way. I somehow think this is destiny, the way life works, the way things are, the way things will be," he replied just as softly.

He picked her up, carried her to his room, and laid her on the bed.

While she lay there, he unbuttoned her slacks, slowly pulled the zipper down, then slid her pants off. She lifted her body up to facilitate the removal. He glided his hands softly across her cheeks as he finished. He unclasped the small hooks on the front of her brassiere and laid each cup to the side. Her more than ample breasts fell only slightly apart, confirming their perkiness as they mostly stood out, with nipples erect. Ted cupped one breast in his hand while he leaned into the other nipple, sucking it gently and flicking it with his tongue. Her abdomen rose as before, this time muscles contracting with desire. She pulled his head tighter into her breast, wanting to be aroused by a little more pressure. He bit her nipple with tightly pursed lips causing the perfect effect of weight, but without pain, her moan lingered, and he took it as a sign of approval.

He lifted her shoulders up and finished removing her bra. Chris lay there fully exposed and very aroused by her vulnerability. While he stood next to her, she reached up to pull his shorts down. He was not wearing underwear, and his manhood, half erect, hung out and pulsed. She grabbed and pulled the appendage toward her, stroking it lightly and gently. Ted's shaft grew instantly larger, longer, and stiffer.

He leaned over and straddled her midsection. He laid his weight on her and held her arms above her head, kissing her lips and chin and moving to her neck. He continued kissing down to her shoulder and then to her chest. More kisses rained down on her breasts. Then, releasing her arms, he moved to her abdomen. With her arms free, she ran her fingers through his hair and guided his head down farther. He kissed her in places she longed to have kissed, and tremors ran through her body over and over, like a stream feeding a river; her juices flowed. She gulped for air between moans of bliss. She pulled his head back up to hers and kissed him feverishly, probing with her tongue, tasting him and herself, and then gently sucking his tongue. He placed himself between her legs and fumbled to apply the condom but was finally successful, and she begged him to be inside her quickly. She was well lubricated from the foreplay, and his covered manliness slowly pushed its way into her without pain. She could feel her vagina stretch slightly as his shaft became fully engorged and swollen. They undulated until the undulation became matched with movement, which aroused her beyond control.

Her legs wrapped behind him, and she tightened them to force him in as deeply as she could, simultaneously compressing the muscles of her abdomen to gain all the feeling of his skin rubbing back and forth and in and out. They were both gasping and moaning, and she screamed at the height of her orgasm. Hearing the sensual outcry from his partner, Ted could no longer contain himself, and his own orgasm was long and draining. When finished, he let his weight fall on her and then rolled off to the side as both were spent.

"Ted! That was wonderful," she said, still out of breath.

"I couldn't have said it better, was everything ok, was anything missing?" Ted asked.

"Well, there's probably more I've fantasized about, but that can come later if you want."

"Well, it's probably a long day tomorrow; we should get some rest.

Under the circumstances, you could just stay in this bed unless you want more privacy."

"This is just fine." She snuggled up to him and quickly fell asleep. Ted reached over and turned off the light.

Chapter 9

They were up the next morning, bright and early. A shower, toast, and coffee, in that order.

"I haven't slept that well in days," she told him.

"I must admit, I feel the same way, Chris."

"Are you sure you can come with me to work?" She asked.

"I'm here to please, ma'am."

"You've done plenty of pleasing so far," she said, giving him a big hug and kiss.

They arrived at her work and pulled into the parking lot as a police car pulled out. The cop and his partner both waved at Ted as they passed. Ted had driven five miles to her work and knew he was being followed by an unmarked patrol car. However, things appeared safe enough for now.

They entered an elegant black five-story building and went to the elevator. Chris was employed by a travel agency on the third floor. The lobby to her office was fronted by large glass panels. She and Ted entered the front door. No one was at the reception desk.

"That's strange. Shelly's not at her desk and is usually here by now."

"Well, it's Monday; maybe she had a wild weekend," Ted said as he eased his revolver out from under the back of his shirt.

Chris saw his move and started back toward the door. They heard movement from down the hallway, and a young girl popped up from around the hall. Ted quickly slid his gun back under his shirt.

Shelly saw Chris by the door.

"Gees Chris, I didn't think you'd be in today with all that's going on with you. It's all over the newspaper. Channel 5 news was at your apartment, but they couldn't find you, and the cops weren't saying anything." She stopped suddenly and looked at Ted.

"Who's this guy?" Shelly asked, slightly startled,

"Shelly, this is my ah... police escort, Ted. Ted, this is Shelly, our receptionist."

"Nice to meet you, Ted," Shelly said with a broad grin, realizing just now how young and handsome he was.

"Same here, Shelly."

"Shelly, Ted's going to hang around while I get some work done,"

"Cool, he can hang around up here with me," Shelly said with a purr.

"Well, Ma'am, I really need to keep an eye on Miss Baker."

"Ok, but please don't call me ma'am, Just Shelly," again with a purr.

"We'll be at my desk if there are any calls."

Christine sat at her desk, and Ted walked around the office. Finally, Chris' boss came in and saw her.

"Chris, I thought you would call. You didn't have to come in today. I saw what happened on the news. You must be upset with this."

"No, Mr. Richards, I'm fine."

"No, I mean, I can't afford you being here or talking to customers."

"Really, I'm fine. I can take care of my customers, really!"

"I'm sorry, Chris, I need you to go home. I think it would be better."

Ted came to the door when he heard the argument. He stood by the door till Mr. Richards finished. Mr. Richards turned to leave and was startled when he saw Ted. Ted held up his badge and introduced himself.

"Well, that's fine. Nice to meet you. I was just explaining to Chris that she needs to stay away until this is over. I don't need the disruption in the office,"

Ted looked at Chris, her eyes were moist, but she was not yet crying.

"I'll be here when you're ready to go," Ted told her.

Chris grabbed her purse and jacket and got up to leave. Mr. Richards moved out of her way. She walked stiffly to the lobby and straight out the door. Shelly had heard the discussion and didn't look up.

Out of the office, she headed to the elevator. Ted trailed behind.

"Asshole!" She whispered.

Ted said nothing, only waited. He knew she was hot and stewing. He was correct in thinking this was not the time to start a conversation.

In the building lobby, she looked at Ted and said, "can we go home now?"

"Certainly, Chris, whatever you need."

They drove the five miles back to his apartment. Ted phoned in the change of plans to the lead detective.

"Ted, you need to return to the precinct and bring Ms. Baker with you." The detective said nervously.

"Will do, be there in twenty. Anything I need to know?"

"

Only to be careful, Ted,"

"Roger, that." Ted hung up and said nothing.

Arriving at the station, Ted parked close to the door and looked around carefully before letting Chris out of the car. There were a few other squad cars and some uniformed officers walking to and from the station. He was slightly on edge because of what the detective had said.

"It looks clear Chris; let's go in."

Ted escorted her to the detective who had called, and then the detective and his partner led them to a private room. Chris and Ted sat down.

"What's going on Ted? Why are we here?" Chris said, starting to lose her nerve.

"Ms. Baker," the detective said as he and his partner took a seat at the table.

"Ms. Baker, we have been investigating Jason. We haven't been able to find him in the city. We had the Chicago police go to his last known address, which in this case was his mother's house. Chris froze in terror; she knew her mother was going to Chicago to see her sister.

"Oh, my god, is my mother alright? She was going there to see her sister. Please tell me she's ok!"

"Your mother is fine. Ironically, Chicago PD showed up at the house at the same time as your mother. Your Aunt, however, was not so fortunate. She was found dead and had been dead for some weeks. We're not sure how she died, but someone wrapped her in plastic. So, we assume, to keep the smell down. Forensics may tell us who was involved, and of course, her son Jason is our number one suspect."

Chris sighed as she heard the news about her mother. She knew extraordinarily little about her aunt, and it still confounded her about being left all her estate, whatever the amount.

"We'd like a DNA sample from you because of your relationship with your cousin Jason. It could help us make the connection to his complicity."

"Sure, I'll do anything to help."

A forensics tech came in and took Chris's sample. Chris further questioned whether Ted would be allowed to maintain his presence with her.

"Normally, we would not assign an around-the-clock guard. But it seems this Jason may have perpetrated multiple homicides; he certainly meets the criteria for a psychopath. So, with that in mind and with your approval, we'll leave Ted in place."

"Well, I certainly approve!" she said, trying to stay meek.

The detective looked at Ted and told him to stay alert. "This guy's a character, and I don't know where he is, what motive drives him, or what I think he would do next. He's a total wild card, and this is no joke. And it's absolutely a lethal combination."

"Got it, and I'd like to get some body armor, and weapons upgrade if it's ok?"

"Good thinking Ted. I'll call down and approve it. Be careful out there."

Ted took Chris with him down to the equipment room and had her sized for a bulletproof vest. He did the same and signed for a nine-millimeter Glock with three extra clips. Chris turned in front of the mirror in the hallway.

"Does this thing really work, Ted; it seems awfully thin?"

"It'll work really well when you need it. Let's hope we don't."

They got in his car and drove back to his house. Ted had a few minutes to ponder his future with this girl. He, without a doubt, was falling in love, but how did she really feel about him? Was it only his current position as a protector, or did they really have chemistry?

Chapter 10

They pulled up to his apartment, and again Ted perused the lot before letting Chris get out of his car. Seeing nothing out of the ordinary, they went in. They took the elevator to the third floor and exited into the hallway. Ted led the way to his door; seeing nothing out of the ordinary, he unlocked the door and went in, looking around. Ted called for Chris to come into the apartment. She didn't respond. Chris was waiting in the hallway when Jason appeared at the door across the hall. She gasped. He held his gun, pointed at her, and put his finger to his lips, calling for her to be silent. She was transfixed on the barrel of his gun. Self-defense classes were one thing, but this was entirely different. This was the real deal. She was frozen in horror at the fact that she could die at any moment. She heard Ted call for her to come inside. Jason approached slowly, now turning his weapon toward the open door of Ted's apartment. If she didn't warn Ted, he would be the next victim of this deranged killer.

Her mind settled on the question of whether or not she really loved Ted. She could try to run, or she could warn Ted. Love won over. As Jason drew near, he was close enough to reach. She threw all her weight into him while grabbing at his gun. At the same time, she let out a scream to let Ted know there was trouble. Jason fell back, struggling with her as she held his hands, pointing the gun in the air.

Ted heard the scream, and his Glock was in hand and ready in the two seconds it took to reach the door. He saw Chris struggling with Jason. They were tangled, dancing with death in the hall. He tried to take aim, but the struggle caused him to be cautious for fear of hitting Chris. Ted lunged for Jason striking him in the head with his Glock and pushing Chris away simultaneously. Chris fell to the floor, only feet from the two men.

The fight was intense, both men struggling for supremacy over the other. Each man's free hand held the wrist of the hand holding the gun. Jason managed to slam Ted's hand against a door frame. Ted's gun went flying away. Now Ted had a free hand with which to grapple with Jason. He hit Jason in the side with the fist of his free arm, hoping desperately to break a rib or at least cause him a lot of pain. Instead, Jason twisted and got his own weapon close enough to pull the trigger. The shot went off, and Ted buckled and flew backward.

Jason aimed his gun at Ted, who was lying on the floor. Jason never pulled the trigger. A nine-millimeter slug penetrated the side of his skull, entering discretely on one side, but with the slug tumbling and separating, it blew out much of his brain while exiting explosively out the other. There was no longer enough gray matter in his head to tell his trigger finger what to do. Jason slumped to the floor.

Chris dropped Ted's gun and crawled, crying, over to Ted. She held his head in her hands and begged him not to leave her. She felt around for the wound but found no blood; confused, she started crying again and calling his name while shaking him.

"Ted, please wake up. I need you. I... I... I love you.

" Ted groaned. "I told you this vest works really well when you need it," struggling to get his breath back.

"I love you too," he added while holding his chest.

She squeezed him tightly; he winced but said nothing.

Chapter 11

Ted was taken to the hospital and released with only one slightly fractured rib. Needless to say, the body armor did its job. Jason was bagged and tagged and sent to the morgue. Chris and Ted went back together to the precinct to debrief. Sitting in his office, Ted and Chris got the wrap-up from the captain.

"Good news is no one else was killed besides your aunt and her son. Jason is dead, and the world is a little safer now. You realize that you saved my officer's life, don't you?"

"We can just call that payback, Captain," she said.

"Well, I must explain one final note to you, and you'll have to take this up with your mother. Forensics came back with their report. It appears that Jason was not your cousin. He was your brother."

"Chris' mouth fell open, dumbfounded. How can that be?"

"It looks like you were given up for adoption by Jason's mother; her sister adopted you. This is one reason you were inheriting your 'aunt's' estate."

"Final fact to this whole confusing state of affairs, your aunt's estate totals five million dollars. Plenty of motive for Jason to go crazy."

That last detail brought a smile to her face and a twinkle to her eye. She looked at Ted and winked.

"Well, I hope you're not kicking me out of your place now that this is over," Chris said.

"I hope you'll always stay," Ted replied.

The captain, who was still in the room, said, "Yuck, will you two get out of my office."

The Itch Chapter 1

Two very large, muscular, and impeccably dressed men entered Balenna's Italian restaurant and took a position on either side of the entrance. A slight bulge under each man's left arm asked the question of how big a sidearm they might be carrying. They scanned the tables from one side to the other, looking for anything out of place; if there had been, they would have immediately exited the establishment. Instead, not seeing anything out of the ordinary, they held their positions. Some of the dinner guests looked toward the door and the two men; a hush began to settle across the floor.

Jimmy "Don" Longino entered. He too, was dressed in the finest mohair overcoat, silk scarf, and hat. Next to him was the adorable Mrs. Longino, a middle-aged woman that could still be on the cover of any glamour magazine and make younger women feel bad about themselves.

The owner and headwaiter of Balenna's ran quickly up to the new guests, a little too fast; as one of the bodyguards stepped in his way, he faltered back and bowed politely. "Please, this way, your table is ready, Don Longino," the waiter said nervously, eyeing the large bodyguard. With this, the large man stepped aside, and the Don and his wife followed. As they walked to their table, the Don removed his hat and coat and handed them to a bodyguard, then before sitting down, smiled at everyone in the room. All the guests either smiled or nodded. Then, the conversations resumed but at a much lower volume.

The Don and his wife were seated, and one of the bodyguards took a station behind the Don and against the wall while the other remained at the door. The wine was brought, the absolute best, the bottle was uncorked, and the Don took a small taste. "Good," he mused. The waiter, waiting in fear, looked slightly relieved and began pouring two glasses.

"Brenda, the same?" the Don asked his wife.

"Of course, Jimmy, you know why I like to come here."

He looked at the waiter and exclaimed, "The usual." The waiter bowed slightly and hurried off to the kitchen.

Don Longino gently took his wife's hand in his. He felt the soft skin and the warmth of her hand. He looked into her eyes, and his body gave an imperceptible shudder. He couldn't get over how this feeling never went away, even after eighteen years of marriage. His love for this woman never faltered or lessened. He was as madly in love with her today as the day they had first met, perhaps even more. "If only I could spend more time with her," he thought to himself. Nevertheless, he must hold his empire together, and that takes many hours and significant involvement.

The food arrived, and the aroma was overwhelming. The buttery tomato sauce, the fragrant basil, the hint of garlic, and the savory oregano rose in steamy curls around the table. The sauce had been poured gently and sparingly over a bed of angel hair pasta. Brenda Longino let the steam from the plate waft up to her face drawing in the flavor as it rose past her. This was indeed her favorite recipe.

Giorgio Pitt, her favorite cook, had made it. Unknown to the Don, Giorgio had even more recipes that Brenda liked to taste. Giorgio remained discretely in the kitchen, watching unobtrusively through the small window in the kitchen door.

Chapter 2

Giorgio Pittroni had practiced cooking since he was a young boy. His grandfather had taught him many excellent secrets of how to make the food taste as good as it could taste. What spices and herbs were best for which meat and fish. By fifteen, he was mature and had an athletic physique. His aptitude for the culinary arts had brought him in contact with quite a few aristocratic families in the old country and with their daughters as well.

As Giorgio matured, so did his skill and tastes. He found himself more engaged with the wives of the household and less and less interested in the younger women of his own age. His older admirers found him to be easier to talk with and, at least, from an outward appearance, more interested in what they had to say. This ability was fine-tuned along with his cooking. Giorgio understood that both skills could be well rewarded. The rewards were substantial both monetarily and physically.

Unfortunately for Giorgio, the consequences were just as significant. Giorgio found himself on a tramp steamer headed for the United States to escape the wrath of a particular estate owner with a gorgeous middle-aged wife. It was wise of Giorgio to change his name to Pitt to throw investigators off his trail.

Brenda Longino had been a frequent visitor to the restaurant and, on many occasions, looked in on the activity in the kitchen. Yes, her rank as the Don's wife gave her leave to do as she liked. She would wander about, inquiring about the cooks, and wait staff with questions about how they did things and life in general. Her beauty was surpassed only by her friendly personality, and Giorgio picked up on her kindliness from her first question.

Many visits to the kitchen were cause for the friendship to grow, and before long, Giorgio was making unique dishes just for Brenda. Giorgio was twenty-five now and as slender and well-built as when he was eighteen. He cooked for Brenda and pursued her as well, oblivious to the man who was her husband and purveyor of all that took place in the surrounding area, whether it be good or bad. Giorgio plied his skills as convincingly as he had ever done before; the barriers of a well-brought-up, respectable woman began to crumble.

Their first meeting, as was all the rest thereafter, was in the early afternoon. She had gone for an afternoon drive to the spa and insisted that she did not need a driver or an escort. She wound up at a small cafe well outside the city, where her husband's influence did not reach. She enjoyed many an afternoon this way, In Giorgio's tender caress, among other things. Afterward, she would go to the spa, and after a quick workout, she would shower and return home, no one the wiser.

Chapter 3

Giorgio watched through the kitchen door window as the husband and wife ate their dinner; he longed to be near her, if only to brush against her innocently. He immediately had an idea. He saw that they had finished their meal and looked quickly around to see who was serving the dessert. Fredrico was holding a tray of desserts, and streaks of sweat were running down the side of his face. Giorgio had never seen him like this; Fredrico was almost shaking.

"Fredrico, what's wrong? You seem upset; what is it?" he whispered.

"I must take these desserts to the Don's table. What if he doesn't like them?" Fredrico replied.

"Not to worry, I'll take the desserts to the table for you!" Giorgio exclaimed.

Relief washed over Fredrico's face. "You're the best, gratzi, gratzi," Fredrico replied, overcome by his newfound good fortune.

With that, Giorgio took the tray and waited patiently for the signal from the maitre d' to bring the tray.

The signal came, and Giorgio walked through the kitchen door gliding smoothly to the table. "Your dessert tray, Don Longino," he said confidently and without hesitation.

Hearing the voice, Brenda looked up, surprised, almost startled. She looked down again quickly, too quickly.

"Thank you, the deserts look lovely," Brenda noted.

Now, Don Longino was a man of great power, and truly, he had the power of life and death. To become this powerful, you must be able to observe minute details and subtleties and read and interpret what is on people's faces. Giorgio placed the tray on the table, brushing Brenda's arm as he did so. Tingles ran through both their bodies, his from eroticism, hers from abject fear. "He must be crazy, no! Insane," she told herself. All this happened while the Don watched every move and expression, keeping his emotions in check.

Longino watched while Giorgio finished serving the desserts, showing only his usual stern, straight face. Brenda looked up, slightly apprehensive, and smiled at the Don. He returned a small grin. Brenda felt somewhat relieved, thinking the Don had noticed nothing. She would break this affair off as soon as she could see Giorgio again. This was her only thought. Finally, Giorgio returned to the kitchen, and the slight tension at the table eased.

Chapter 4

The Don arranged for his very best investigator to follow Brenda the next day. Loved her, he did, but he must know how serious this association with the cook was with his wife. Yes, he had noticed facial expressions and apprehensions in the voices of the cook and his wife.

Kent Scarilli had been in the service of the Don for many years. His expertise was in following people and observing their most private moments without being noticed himself. This was very handy for the Don to demand service and favor with extortion. The Don knew everyone had secrets, and Kent knew how to find those secrets no matter how deeply buried.

Brenda started out for her afternoon trip to the spa. She looked around before she left and kept watching the entire time she drove. Sure, in her mind, no car had followed her to the café where Giorgio would be waiting. But, unfortunately for Brenda, Kent knew how to easily track her whereabouts without moving very far; he needed only to keep within range of the signal device he had planted under the car. That would keep him well out of sight.

Brenda parked the car just down the street from her destination and, standing by the car's door, took one last look around the block before walking toward the café. She did not see Kent a block away watching her through the high-powered lens of his camera. Brenda entered and took a seat at a booth at the far end of the café. Giorgio was not yet there, but she knew him to be cautious, at least until the other night at the restaurant. Now she had trepidations about his cautiousness and certainly about how his side of this affair had become more than she had ever wanted it to be. She loved her husband, but he was older and less attentive than she needed. She only wanted this affair to be distant, satisfying her libido and fantasy, nothing more.

Chapter 5

Giorgio entered the restaurant from the back door, looking around at the sparsely populated seating area of the small café. He seated himself at the table with Brenda. He moved to hold her hand, and she drew away quickly. He looked into her eyes, and they returned a cold, impersonal stare. Giorgio knew from her gaze that he could never talk his way back into her life. He had stepped past that invisible line drawn by his lover. Perhaps it was unfair that Brenda had not made that line clearer. Maybe life was unfair had he known how deeply he would fall in love with this woman who started out to be only another cougar conquest.

Brenda stared at him with steel blue eyes. Inside she was seething with contempt.

"What did you think you were doing? What was going through your mind?" she said through pursed lips.

"I needed to be near you. I needed to touch you. I needed to know I was in your thoughts," he replied with remorse.

"Giorgio! I didn't know you felt that way, and If Jimmy ever found out about you, I don't want to think what he would do to you. I don't want that to happen," She retorted. "This affair has to end," she finished and began to leave. Giorgio grabbed her hand and forced her back to the table.

"He can't love you as I do. If he did, you wouldn't have needed to look for someone like me. Someone like me, to give you the love and the attention that you have been missing; someone like me, to make you feel like the woman you are, beautiful and alluring," he forced her to hear the words.

Brenda knew the feelings that Giorgio's words described. Nevertheless, Brenda fell in love with Jimmy at a time when he was more attentive, more alive, and far less involved with the family business. Brenda also had enjoyed the lifestyle and never lacked money. However, her life had been far less glamorous as a young woman working as a waitress. High school and college had brought little success to her life, and jobs were hard enough to find. She had no direction to travel and sought life pragmatically, waiting for some sign from above to help her choose a path. Then Jimmy came into the restaurant where she waited tables. He was handsome, with an air of total authority. As she moved from table to table, she could feel his eyes on her. She finally confronted him and asked if he had a problem.

"Yes! Yes, I do. I find that I have never seen anyone as beautiful and graceful as you in the entire city," he told her with solid confidence.

Brenda had heard pickup lines like this before and, at first, was going to tell Jimmy he needed a new one. But looking into his eyes told Brenda that Jimmy was sincere. From that moment on, she knew her path was chosen. Jimmy made the diner a regular stop. He began courting Brenda regularly. Jimmy was tender, patient, and intriguing. Six months later, Jimmy proposed. He presented Brenda with an engagement ring with a diamond as big as she had ever seen. Her heart melted, and she said yes.

Brenda looked up once more at Giorgio.

"It's over, done, finished. I can't see you again. I won't see you again," she said flatly. "Don't try to contact me. It wouldn't be healthy," she finished dryly.

Giorgio released her hand. Brenda got up and left the restaurant. Giorgio grimly left as well; he walked out the back door the same way he had entered.

Chapter 6

Kent removed the micro camera concealed in the wall across the alley opposite the restaurant's rear door. He had anticipated all the escape avenues, but of course, that's why he was so good at his business. He dropped the camera in his pocket and was quickly on his way.

Kent got a trace on Giorgio with little effort. "In Giorgio's line of work, you'd think he would take more precaution from jealous husbands," Kent whispered to himself. Maybe he never had a run-in before, thought the PI. Kent followed him to his apartment one evening after Giorgio got off work. It was a nice neighborhood, not too affluent and not too run-down. This was just the type of neighborhood in which a quiet person would not draw attention to himself. A few days of stakeout told Kent when Giorgio left and when he came home.

Kent watched Giorgio leave for the day and then inconspicuously slipped in the back door and up the stairs to the apartment. Again, with little effort, he picked the lock and let himself in. It was a not-too-large but well-furnished place. The living room was big enough to be comfortable with an expensive couch, two chairs, a coffee table, end tables, and lamps. A modern computer table was in one corner, and a small dining area was next to the small gourmet kitchen at the other end of the room. A spacious and tastefully decorated bathroom separated what looked to be two bedrooms. The first bedroom looked as though Cupid might have decorated it. Silk seemed to abound everywhere. This was probably for the erotic fulfillment of guests. Kent opened the next door to find no bedroom but a well-equipped exercise room. It appears that Giorgio worked at keeping himself fit to maintain his non-cooking skills at peak efficiency.

Kent placed a few bugs throughout the house, including a bedroom camera, then left as quietly as he had entered.

Chapter 7

Jimmy got up from the breakfast table and kissed Brenda on the forehead in passing. Brenda smiled and gave him the typical have a beautiful day salutation. He smiled back and headed for the Lincoln parked in the four-car attached garage.

Still in her robe, Brenda headed upstairs while the maid cleared the breakfast table. Standing in front of the mirror of her dressing room, Brenda dropped her robe. Naked, she stared at her body in the mirror. She was slender and trim, certainly well fit for her age. Years of relentless daily exercise had kept her looking exactly how she wanted to look. A few age lines in the face and around her eyes were inevitable, but short of that, her diet and exercise routines were working just fine. The only shortcoming was that the same regimen also kept her libido heightened. The itch was back, and she needed scratching.

Giorgio picked up the phone and heard Brenda's soft voice at the other end of the line. "G, I need to see you," she said softly. Giorgio wanted to confront her about their separation but did not want to start a controversy when she sounded so vulnerable. However, he was more than willing to set aside his male ego for his male satisfaction.

"Certainly, my love, come over to my place. I'll make some cappuccinos, and we can talk without being bothered," he said as convincingly as ever.

She hesitated for a moment, wondering if this was the best idea, but Giorgio's voice spoke of quiet and privacy with great conviction, and she felt assured that everything would be fine. "I'll be there in an hour," she answered and hung up.

Within the hour, Brenda arrived at his apartment. Her personal key let her in with ease, and she padded down the hall to the corner apartment and again let herself in and returned the key to her purse. She could hear Giorgio in the bedroom singing to himself, a soft Italian song he often would sing when he was happy. She had heard it many times. He would whisper the song in her ear when she was at the height of a beautiful sexual climax. He never told her exactly the words but insisted the song was about love and pleasure.

Giorgio came out of the bedroom; a look of surprise lit his face when he saw her. Still, with trepidation, he hesitated, unsure of her intentions or feelings. Finally, she moved toward him, and they embraced firmly, warmth exchanging between them. She was crying at this point. Guilt, shame, and desire overwhelmed her all at once, and she could not hold them back. From deep inside, Giorgio could feel her trembling and knew this was his queue to put on his best performance. He would be his gentlest and kindest and would be fulfilling his needs as well as hers before the hour was up. She, indeed, was his greatest triumph.

An hour later, they both lay in the silk-covered bed, breathing now recovered. She smiled as she stared up at the ceiling. There was no room for guilt or shame; her fulfillment was as complete as any woman could ask for; Giorgio was an expert. He knew exactly what she wanted and precisely when. It was as if he could read her mind.

Brenda got dressed as Giorgio watched from the bed. Brenda felt his eyes on her and dressed slower and more deliberately. It made her tingle like an aftertaste from a sweet, creamy dessert. When she was finished, she laid a small box on the table, leaned over, and gave him a long kiss,

"I'll be in touch...very soon when the time is right, and from now on, don't do anything stupid to ruin this," she said and left the apartment.

Chapter 8

Kent had watched the entire event as the camera transmitted each provocative moment of the hour-long lovemaking. He now sat back from the screen, perspiration running down the side of his face. Panting heavily, his own manhood had just now started to recede as the seconds passed. If the "Don" had seen him staring with desire at his wife, he would have had a bullet through his temple. As it was, he would have to crop and clip the video into a series of incriminating but discrete poses to avoid insulting the Don. It had to be enough to confirm a suspicion, but not humiliate him or his family. Kent was having second thoughts about ever having put the camera in the bedroom.

Jimmy's office was at the farthest back reaches of the furniture store. Furniture that was European-made and that would sell for ridiculously unreasonable prices had, in fact, been doubled. The prices listed on each piece kept browsers from going past the first twenty pieces in the front of the store; of course, that was the intent. From his office, the Don conducted all business transactions. The pulse of the Family quickened or slowed by each action of the Don. Sometimes contracts are made, and sometimes alliances. On other days, it was merely money that flowed through the electronics on the Don's desk, Always seen as perfectly legitimate.

A small bell attached to the front door gave out its little schoolroom ting. The man at the front recognized the intruder but looked to another man standing at the back by the Don's office door. This man, in turn, looked toward the Don, who, seeing who it was on his video monitor, gave an approving nod, which in turn was given to the man at the front. The man at the front eased the silenced pistol back into the shoulder holster. Recognized or not, the intruder would not have made it but a few more feet if the proper signal had not come.

Chapter 9

Giorgio showered and dressed. Looking down at the package she had left, he picked it up and began to unwrap it. It was hefty for its size, and he could not guess what it might be. Lifting the lid on the box, his eyes lit up, and a smile spread across his face. The watch was gold, very, very gold. The custom-made Rolex fit elegantly on his wrist. She had gifted him smaller bracelets and a ring or two but never something as expensive as this.

Chapter 10

Kent stood nervously by the Don's desk.

"I have the evidence you were looking for, Mr. Longino," Kent said as he laid the manila envelope on the desk.

"I wasn't looking for evidence, Kent; I was looking for peace of mind," Jimmy replied sullenly.

"Yes sir, I'm sorry," Kent said hesitantly.

"Don't be. You'll get your payment on the way out. That will be all!"

Kent backed away slowly, with a slight bow, not knowing quite how to exit the room gracefully. Finally, by the door, he turned and left. In the hallway, a large man reached into his suit coat. Kent thought, "this is it," I've done the wrong thing. I should have turned the job down." But, he thought, that wouldn't have been an alternative either. Then, as the hallway began to spin, Kent saw an envelope in the man's hand, not a gun. The large man handed him the envelope and stepped back, leaving the hallway open for Kent to pass. Kent left as quickly and quietly as he could but was still a little dizzy from the elevated blood pressure that he was sure someday would kill him.

Jimmy stared at the envelope on the table for a long time. He was thinking of the good times, the vacations, the holidays, the evenings, and the nights. They were fewer and fewer as the years had passed. Where had all the time gone? Finally, he reached over and picked up the envelope, opening it as slowly as possible, wishing with all his heart that this day would disappear from existence. He started to slide the photographs out from the darkness of the envelope.

Chapter 11

Brenda was busy with the caterer, making final preparations for Jimmy's surprise birthday party. It was all she could do to contain herself. She wasn't big at keeping secrets, ordinary secrets anyway. She just hoped the rest of the family could keep their mouths shut. Jimmy had never had anything but quiet suppers on his birthday and would never guess, on his own, what was up.

Chapter 12

Jimmy decided not to pull the photos out of the envelope. After all, they had been together for almost twenty years. Perhaps, this is the kind of thing that a married woman needs from time to time. The PI's nervousness let Jimmy know he had the evidence to verify what was happening. Still, the affair showed a lack of respect on the cook's part. This he could not tolerate. Jimmy made a few more phone calls and set in motion the demise of the handsome young culinary 'asshole.'

Chapter 13

Demi Saline was slim, trim, and tight. Her face was as good-looking as they came. She divorced her husband of twenty years and took with her most of his estate. Her ex-husband had often visited her and beat her senseless more than once. Demi was a friend of Jimmy through her father's close association with the family. Last year, she called on Jimmy for a favor, knowing that favors must be repaid.

Fredrico Saline's body lay on the floor, dead in his apartment. Apparently, he had committed suicide. Obviously, for Demi, there would be no more beatings.

Demi had been feeling ill lately and had been to see the doctor. She sat in the examining room, waiting for the doctor to return with the test results. Waiting much longer than she thought it would take, she dressed and was about to leave when the doctor tapped on the door.

"Come in," she said, only slightly agitated by the wait.

"I'm terribly sorry about the delay," the doctor said apologetically. He looked sullen as he apologized, and that gave Demi pause for concern.

The atmosphere in the exam room became thick with anxiety.

"I had to make sure," the doctor began.

Demi heard the excuse, and her heart sank; she fell as gracefully as she could into the exam room chair. As much as she had exercised and eaten properly, staying trim, she felt her other transgressions may have caught up with her. She felt awful lately, really terrible, which was the reason for this medical evaluation. She looked up at the doctor with tearful, questioning eyes.

"I'm very sorry, Ms. Saline, you have AIDS," her stomach knotted further than it already was, and she bent over in the chair, crying heavily. Through her tears, she recalled the many men and women she had been intimate with both before and after her divorce. She had not been very cautious, giving way to her pleasures thoughtlessly.

Because the Don had granted her favors, Demi was on a list of closely watched people who may be asked to return a favor. Jimmy was made aware of her condition almost before she had left the doctor's office. With this information, Jimmy had already figured out a fitting punishment for the young cook that had entered his life.

A week later, Demi left Jimmy's office. She was fully aware of the favor that now must be repaid. She never in a million years thought repayment would be by something she thoroughly enjoyed. After the doctor's diagnosis, she felt celibacy would be the only alternative lifestyle available. That was not something she was looking forward to for the rest of her short-to-be-lived life. The Don's request was a turn of events she never saw coming. Nevertheless, she jumped at the chance to repay him.

Chapter 14

Demi Saline winced as the sunlight bounced off the gold watch as Giorgio slid his hand across the table to embrace hers.

"That watch is beautiful," she said to him.

"What this? It's just a little trinket that I wear from time to time," he replied.

"Well, that's the most beautiful trinket I've ever seen," she said admiringly.

"Not as beautiful as you," He returned, trying very hard not to add "trinket" to the sentence.

Demi was an extreme cougar. Slender, sensual, soft-spoken, and intelligent; just the kind of middle-aged prize Giorgio was after. Giorgio had gone to a local nightclub for some socialization. He got a drink from the bar and was leisurely walking to the edge of the dance floor when he spotted Demi. She had everything Giorgio looked for in a target. Middle-aged, well-dressed, great figure, beautiful face, and ample breasts. She was nearly a ten in his book of 'Cougars.' Demi knew who Giorgio was, what he looked like, and the places he visited, Jimmy's information on him was very detailed. She made sure Giorgio saw her and made sure she gave him an approving smile.

Demi allowed Giorgio to continue with his flattery. Giorgio had found her to be without a husband and very well-to-do. This meant there could be some lovely gifts in the future if he played his cards right. After a light meal and a few more drinks, Giorgio speculated he would be hanging this prize on his wall.

He played his cards, and Giorgio took Demi in every conceivable way imaginable. Demi as well taught him a few tricks of her own. They went on like this a couple of days a week for the next month. Demi was taking steroids and painkillers to keep up her stamina while voraciously copulating with Giorgio. If Demi had anything to give, Giorgio was getting all of it. Gifts came from Demi in the form of some costly jewelry.

However, Giorgio wanted more. He looked at his Rolex and thought, "Well, this is really nice, but you can't drive it," he thought to himself. He advanced that thought to how great it would be to have a Porsche. He looked at the Rolex again and wondered when Brenda might be calling. He knew that Brenda could never supply a car, but he was in the mood for a change of pace. Demi was having a rest day; maybe he would give Brenda a call.

Chapter 15

Brenda answered the phone and heard Giorgio's soft voice at the other end. Her juices started flowing, and she looked around to see if anyone else was nearby.

"I've been waiting patiently for you to call me. I couldn't wait any longer!" he said decisively.

"I know; I'm sorry, I've been busy planning my husband's party," she hesitantly replied.

"I need to see you. I need to touch you," he ambitiously said to her.

As much as Brenda knew she should not continue this conversation, her knees began to weaken, and she had to sit down. There was a slight tremor in her stomach as the forbidden fruit became easier to pluck.

"Where could we meet, Giorgio? It has been too long," she whispered.

"My place tonight, eight o'clock," he answered.

They both agreed and disconnected, then the phones made a distinctive 'click' that neither party heard.

Seven o'clock approached as Giorgio was getting ready for Brenda's visit. A light knock on the door surprised Giorgio, but he just assumed Brenda was a little early. He didn't even look through the peephole in the door to verify who was knocking. Two things suddenly struck him as he swung open the door. The first was the thought that Brenda had her own key, and the second was a fist that landed squarely in his face. He rolled backward and onto the coffee table, smashing it to pieces and trying desperately to get up, and having no success, a hand reached out to help him. He looked up at the hand.

"You're going to kill me, aren't you?" he said, almost crying.

"No, No, Mr. Pitt, I don't kill people," the man said. "But sometimes they wish they were dead," he continued. "It's not good business," he finished.

Giorgio suspiciously grabbed the hand, thinking another fist was coming, but the hand and the person behind it helped him to his feet.

The man, well dressed and of average height and weight, merely said." Sorry about that old chap, but I needed you to know that what I'm about to tell you is very serious, and there won't be any discussion about it." Giorgio, holding his nose and wincing in pain, could only shake his head in agreement.

"Mr. Pitt, please listen to these instructions carefully. We know all about you. It is obvious that most of your income comes solely from your looks and your charmingly persuasive dialog," the man began. "Consider the cost of facial reconstruction, to say nothing of what it will take to repair your vocal cords should you not do what you are told," the man finished.

Giorgio, horrified, wondering why he wasn't dead, could only look at the man's face to see that he was serious, after which he closed his eyes in agony. Again, Giorgio shook his head in agreement.

"You will call Mrs. Longino and tell her you have to cancel tonight's arrangement, something has come up, and you will be out of town till further notice," the man explained, as he strolled around the apartment as if he was looking for something else. "Understood?" The man asked emphatically.

For the third time, Giorgio shook his head in agreement but much more vigorously. "All right then, I hope we do not meet again." He concluded and left the apartment.

Giorgio, for want of what else to do, called Brenda and said to her what he was told to say. He disconnected and went to the bathroom to clean the blood off his face. On the way to get ice from the frig, someone knocked on the door. Fear ran through him, and he hesitated to go anywhere near the door.

"Giorgio, are you home? It's me, Demi!"

Hearing Demi's voice, he was relieved. He opened the door, and Demi cringed, seeing the bruises on his face, the swollen nose, and the bags under his eyes turning a slight shade of purple.

"Come on in, Demi," he said. "I still need to clean the place up a bit."

"What happened?" she asked. "Just the jealous husband of an old girlfriend," he said for want of any better excuse.

"Poor baby, lie down, and I'll clean things up, and then, after that, we can play doctor," she said invitingly.

Hearing that and the tone of her voice, the swelling was not relegated to just his nose.

Chapter 16

After hearing Giorgio's pitiful excuse, Brenda hung up and laid the cell phone down on the table. She sighed and thought to herself that it must be for the best. The surprise party was only two days away, and there were still a few more details to finish up.

Ironically, the party would be held at Balenna's, where this whole affair seemed to have begun. No other place would have the privacy or the intimacy for Jimmy's birthday party.

The big day came, and all the guests had arrived early as planned. The party was a remarkable success. There was tasty food, wine, and music for dancing! Jimmy rose, took Brenda's hand, and walked her to the dance floor. He slipped one arm around her midsection and raised the other arm, outstretched, to hold her hand. As he did, his sleeve slid back to reveal a beautiful custom Rolex. Brenda was stunned but remained demur as she always did. She knew that her husband was aware of things, but just how much she did not know until now. Then, she realized why Giorgio had canceled and knew he would never call again.

She could only hope that he was still alive.

Jimmy never said another thing about the affair. He knew he was partly to blame. The office he held in the family had taken him away from her all too often. Jimmy promised himself it would never happen again. He loved her too much.

Chapter 17

Demi and Giorgio stayed together for the next year. The swelling in his face went down over time, but his nose never looked the same. He did look good driving around in the candy apple red Porche Demi had presented to him, and it helped his pickup lines when his slightly disfigured nose became a shortcoming.

With her immune system in the shape, it was, Demi's health continued to decline, but as part of her deal with the Don, she never told Giorgio about her medical condition. They stopped seeing each other because Demi no longer had the strength to pursue any sexual satisfaction with the magnificent gigolo. Giorgio continued his sexual conquests with a few other women but fell prey to an infection, and his own declining immune system took its toll. Early the following year, Demi and Giorgio died within months of each other.

***

Jimmy would never again let Brenda's itch go unscratched by anyone but himself.

Don't miss out!

Visit the website below and you can sign up to receive emails whenever J.J. Smiley publishes a new book. There's no charge and no obligation.

https://books2read.com/r/B-A-NBSE-EJUAC

BOOKS 2 READ

Connecting independent readers to independent writers.

About the Author

Disappointed with titles that I read or watched in the theatre, it was time to write my own adventures. Just writing for personal pleasure at first and then publishing, has now become a joyful pastime.

My wife who is always watching my back convinced me to go to press.

www.ingramcontent.com/pod-product-compliance
Lightning Source LLC
Chambersburg PA
CBHW031438130726
47989CB00003B/1196